THE ADVENTURES OF CHLOE
THE RV DOG AND HER FRIENDS

May The Lord Bless
&
Keep you!
Justine & Chloe

THE ADVENTURES OF CHLOE THE RV DOG AND HER FRIENDS

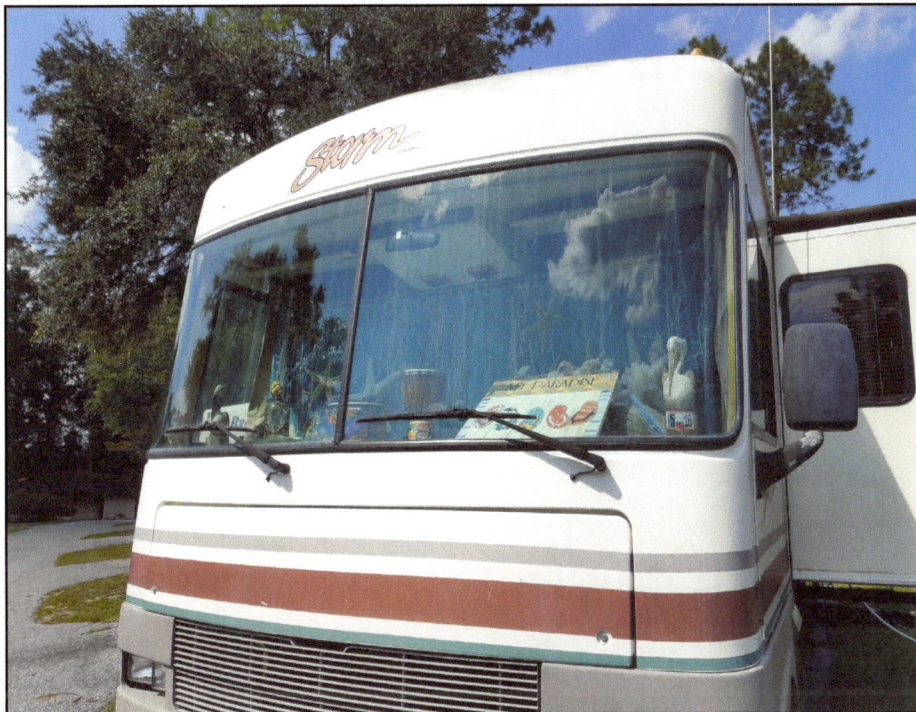

Justine Webster

ELM HILL

A Division of
HarperCollins Christian Publishing

www.elmhillbooks.com

The Adventures of Chloe
The RV Dog and Her Friends

Published in Nashville, Tennessee, by Elm Hill, an imprint of Thomas Nelson. Elm Hill and Thomas Nelson are registered trademarks of HarperCollins Christian Publishing, Inc.

Elm Hill titles may be purchased in bulk for educational, business, fund-raising, or sales promotional use. For information, please e-mail SpecialMarkets@ThomasNelson.com.

Library of Congress Cataloging-in-Publication Data

Library of Congress Control Number: 2018960004

ISBN 978-0-310103752 (Paperback)
ISBN 978-0-310103769 (Hardbound)
ISBN 978-0-310103776 (eBook)

Hello! My name is Chloe. I live in an RV with my owner. She is a very nice lady who has seen a lot of pain in her life. After surviving being hit by a semi, cancer and chemo, and a divorce, she rescued me from a shelter. I was gonna be her therapy dog, and companion, to help her find hope and happiness again. Boy, is she in for a treat with me! I would have loved to chase squirrels, but she just holds on to the leash real tight. Ugh! How is a dog supposed to have any fun? I love this life and I meet a lot of new friends in our travels.

Here are a few of them...

You gotta meet Paris! Some call her the gambler! She is quite a card player. She lives with a beautiful lady who teaches people how to swim for a living. I am not sure if Paris can float, but she is a joy to have around. She always has a card under her paw ready to try her hand. If you see her, tell her to know when to hold them and when to fold them.

Play on...

One of my friends is Penny. She is adorable and loving. She has a brother named Maximilian. He is a ham! A little camera shy hiding under the blanket but a blast to know. They live with a gentleman who works to keep people safe around water. They love it when he comes home and they greet him with lots of kisses and love. Oh, this reminds me I need to go give my master a kiss so she knows I love her! She is eating too and I love it when she shares with me. Hang loose, Penny and Maximilian.

See ya later...

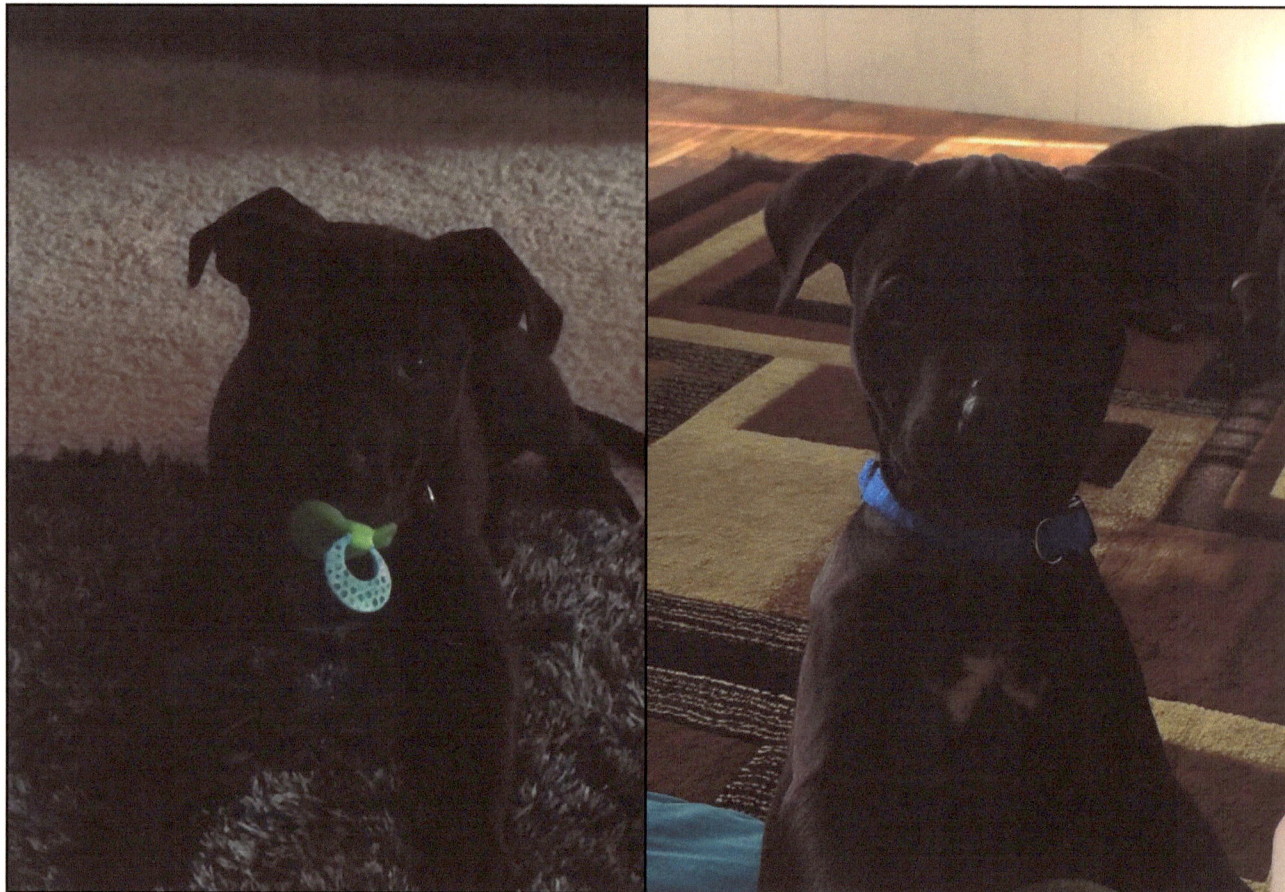

My next two friends Noah and Mia are funny! They live with a beautiful family in a house where our camper used to be. Mia looks so funny with that binky in her mouth what a baby! Yuck, a binky! Lol! As for Noah, now that there is a different story. He is a character! He has enough energy for all of us. He is adventurous, loving to run and play. Wow! What a life to be surrounded by all that love and care. Oops, I forgot to keep my kibble off the floor. Hide, everyone! I hear her coming!

Rock on, Noah and Mia...

You will love my next friend. Her name is Bailey. She lives with a beautiful couple who spoil her silly. She is a diva, always getting her hair done and getting all fancied up for different holidays! She even has a raincoat for when it rains! Gotta love her! She always smells real good to not like her, always pretty, taking it from her beautiful master. She even saves her owner from snakes when they show up. Wow! Where can I hide? Not me!

Always a diva...

Uh-uh, I forgot one! Her name is Candice! Such a happy dog! She lives in a house full of babies. Her owners are raising a family and have little feet pattering around all the time. That doesn't bother her a bit. She loves them and protects them from harm. She loves babies. Not me —they pull my ears –ouch! Way to go, Candice! You're my hero! Only you could be a full-time babysitter.

Stroll on...

Let me introduce you to my three new friends. Left to right: Paxton the quiet one, Zoe the playful one, and Oliver the protector and defender. They live in a beautiful home with owners who have beautiful hearts full of love for all. They live lives full of leisure and pampering. I am so blessed to be able to call them my friends.

Play on my pampered friends...

Let me tell you about two of the sweetest girls I have ever met! They live at Lake Harmony RV Park. Their owners are two of the sweetest people you would ever meet just like their pets. They are full of smiles and laughter that is infectious. Dahlia, now she has it made –her feet never touch the ground. She gets carried to her pee spot. Wow! I wish my feet didn't get wet. Daisy, now she would do anything for a treat! Let me tell you I am glad they touched my life.

Stop by and say hi...

Ah! My sweet friend Maureen. How I do miss her! Her family misses her dearly too. She went to doggy heaven. Such a pretty and loving friend. She had a gentle heart and a love beyond compare. So happy to be walked and so joyous to make your day. She is now running down streets of gold playing fetch with Jesus 'til we see her again someday. Play on, my mighty friend. We will meet again someday.

Rest in peace...

You gotta meet my buddy Banjo. Talk about chicken – I think he is even afraid of his shadow! His care-taker fluffs hair and does nails for a living. Oh my, does he run when he hears the clippers running. He is a good dog, though. He never makes a mess and always stays in the yard. He is a little crazy if you touch his toys though. He will come after you –believe me I tried. That's OK! Who needs his toy? I have more fun trying to chase squirrels. Stay safe, Banjo!

Oh a chair...hide...

You gotta meet Buddy and Gypsy –they are islanders. Their mama is an island girl. Always working outside making things look beautiful for all to see. She loves her fur babies! Buddy and Gypsy are always at sea, so to speak. Always at the beach, the ocean, or on the dock or the back porch. They love it! Island breezes and quiet sunsets in their loving mama's arms. Warming her feet and loving her bed. Oh yeah. I love being under the covers at bedtime! Yee haw!

Hang loose...

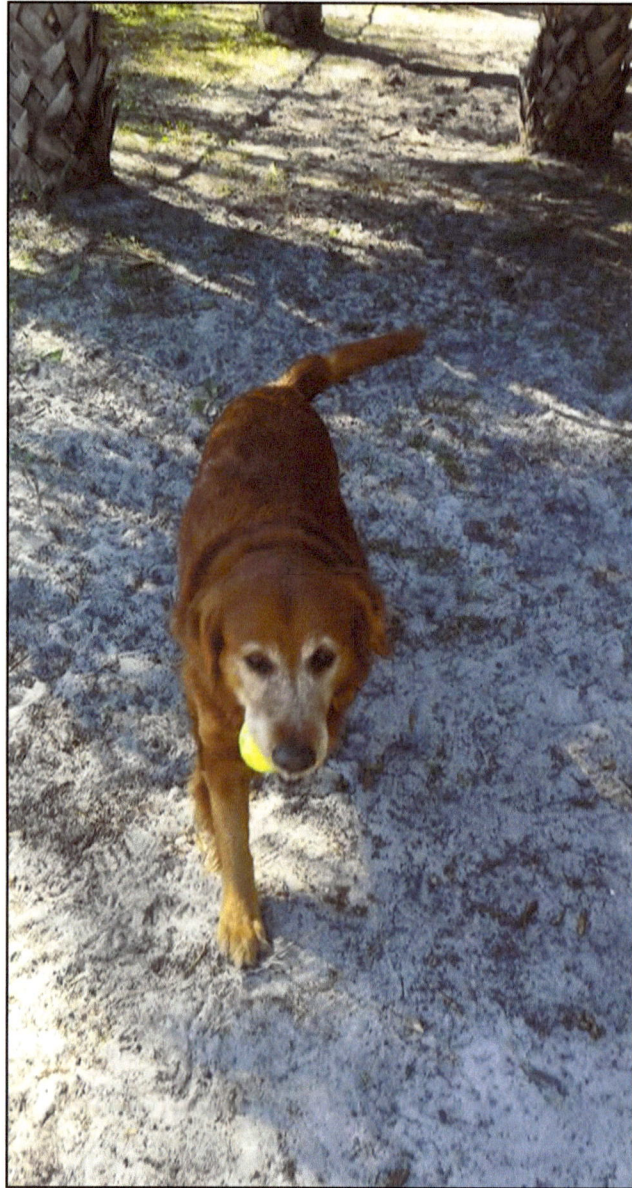

Before I close my stories, I would like to bid adieu to a good ole fella named Maxie. He was a good ole boy. He loved to play a good game of fetch the ball no matter where it landed. He loved the water and his carefree owners. They knew how to live and enjoy life, making it an adventure he would never forget. He is on the other side now, running with ease and catching every ball Jesus throws him. Oh, that glorious day when we all can play ball with Jesus!

Dream on...

Wait 'til you meet Peppy and Roxie. They live with a very crafty lady. She can make a quilt in a day! She is so handy doing all kinds of things. She even paints rocks for people. Boy, do they guard their masters. They bark at me as soon as they see me. Let me tell you I will keep my distance from those two. I think they would whip my butt if they got a hold of me. Well, I'm a lover not a fighter. I go in peace. Is it bedtime yet?

Guard on, guys...

Last but not least is Jake. Someone I have never met but my master has pictures of him and tells me what a good dog he was. He is also in doggy heaven and I guess I will meet him someday. He looks cool like a Mr. T with all those chains. It is sure hard to live up to another bow- wow before you, but I am gonna try. I want to thank my master for loving me and giving me a happy warm place to crash and for always feeding and taking care of me.

Kiss!...Kiss!...Kiss!

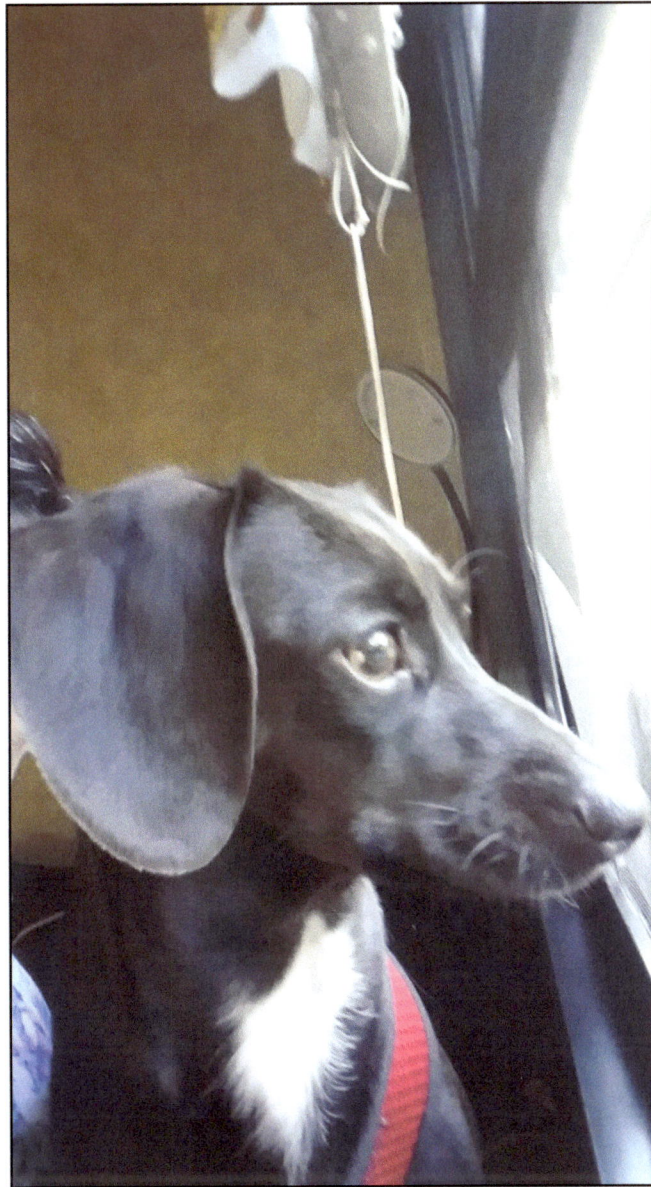

Sorry I missed one: his name is Tip. Talk about a traveling dog– he has been everywhere! His owners are traveling folks. They love it! Seeing the best sights America has to offer. Our great land! His little feet have touched them all. He is carefree and loving every minute of it. Adventure, oh what a life! Someday I hope my master, friend, bed buddy does that. Travel 'til the wheels fall off! Roll on, my friend.

Arrivederci!...

I made two new friends yesterday. Their names are Izzy and Pollyann. They have the kindest masters who have been through a lot like my master. Izzy loves to sit at his masters' boots and is real smart, but Pollyann rules the roost. She sneaks Izzy's toys when he is asleep, to let him know who is boss. They are hilarious, love each other, and have become best friends.

Play on, my friends...

Let me tell you about my new buddies, Bella and Rusty. They are cool! They are balls of fluff, but don't let that fool you: they have a lot of spunk! They live with a lady who helps other people find hope with her words and caring. She is a nurse and a very kind and friendly lady. She loves Bella and Rusty dearly and would be lost without them, just like my master would be without me. They have a great spirit for adventure!

Travel on...

Oh, my! I woke up this morning and realized I forgot about Buddy. We'll just call him cowboy for short. I love that hat! I wish my head was bigger for one. He has a great mom like mine. She loves him to death! Not literally tho! She spoils him and he is quite a character. Calm on the outside but full of energy on the inside. He sure is a mamma's boy! The girls will love that! He is a lovable ball of fun and enjoys every minute of his life. Travel on my good friend.

Yee-Haw...

Wow! Let me tell you about my new friends. We will call them the three amigos – Kayla, Clyde, Carl—and they are really cool! The lady whom they live with is a miracle worker according to my master! She is the best "back cracker" my master has ever met. Stopping my master's pain and helping her to make changes in her life that have helped her heal. I am sure Kayla, Clyde, and Carl are blessed to have her as their master. Always giving them the best home they could ever have. They are awesome!

Si!...Si!...

Wow! You got to meet my new friend Scout. I love his spike. He ventured out the other night on his own and guess what happened? He met Pete the skunk and he was crazy enough to grab Pete's tail. That's right... Man his new perfume is awful. His mommy sure wasn't happy with him when he came romping home either. She bathed him in tomato juice and could not get rid of his new smell. I laughed till my sides hurt. Scout and his masters are really cool. So glad we met.

Romp on...

CPSIA information can be obtained
at www.ICGtesting.com
Printed in the USA
LVHW072044050619
620312LV00004B/12/P

9 780310 103752